Tonkinese Cats as Pets

The Ultimate Guide for Tonkinese Cats

Tonkinese Cats General Info, Purchasing, Care, Cost, Keeping, Health, Supplies, Food, Breeding and More Included!

By Lolly Brown

Copyrights and Trademarks

All rights reserved. No part of this book may be reproduced or transformed in any form or by any means, graphic, electronic, or mechanical, including photocopying, recording, taping, or by any information storage retrieval system, without the written permission of the author.

This publication is Copyright ©2018 NRB Publishing, an imprint. Nevada. All products, graphics, publication, software and services mentioned and recommended in this publication are protected by trademarks. In such instance, all trademarks & copyright belong to the respective owners. For information consult www.NRBpublishing.com

Disclaimer and Legal Notice

This product is not legal, medical, or accounting advice and should not be interpreted in that manner. You need to do your own due-diligence to determine if the content of this product is right for you. While every attempt has been made to verify the information shared in this publication, neither the author, neither publisher, nor the affiliates assume any responsibility for errors, omissions or contrary interpretation of the subject matter herein. Any perceived slights to any specific person(s) or organization(s) are purely unintentional.

We have no control over the nature, content and availability of the web sites listed in this book. The inclusion of any web site links does not necessarily imply a recommendation or endorse the views expressed within them. We take no responsibility for, and will not be liable for, the websites being temporarily unavailable or being removed from the internet.

The accuracy and completeness of information provided herein and opinions stated herein are not guaranteed or warranted to produce any particular results, and the advice and strategies, contained herein may not be suitable for every individual. Neither the author nor the publisher shall be liable for any loss incurred as a consequence of the use and publication, directly or indirectly, of any information presented in this work. This publication is designed to provide information in regard to the subject matter covered.

Neither the author nor the publisher assume any responsibility for any errors or omissions, nor do they represent or warrant that the ideas, information, actions, plans, suggestions contained in this book is in all cases accurate. It is the reader's responsibility to find advice before putting anything written in this book into practice. The information in this book is not intended to serve as legal, medical, or accounting advice.

Foreword

If you ever think that cats are independent and aloof, you have not met a Tonkinese cat yet! This cat boasts to be a playful, social, loving, and active yet a cuddly lap cat you want. This cat breed is generous in showing their love and affection but still uses its mind in whatever activity it is doing.

There are many things you need to know about the Tonkinese cat. We will make sure that you know all the historical information, general knowledge, physical attributes, as well as the health hazards of this cat. We will also familiarize you with Tonkinese cat terms especially in grooming, maintenance, habitat, and nutrition.

Table of Contents

Introduction 1
Chapter One: Biological and Historical Data 3
　Taxonomy 4
　How Did Tonkinese Cats Came About? 4
　Biological Facts 6
　　Quick Facts 7
Chapter Two: Keeping Tonkinese Cats 9
　Behavior, Characteristics, and Temperament 10
　Socializing with Children and Other Pets 11
　Is this the Right Breed for You? 12
　Cat Permits and Regulations 13
　　Licensing for Cats in the U.S. 14
　　Licensing for Cats in the U.K. 16
　　Travel Permits for Cats 16
　Financial Aspects of Cat Keeping 17
　　Average Price of the Tonkinese Cats 18
　　Cat Accessories 18
　　Veterinary Expenses 20
Chapter Three: Selecting the Right Tonkinese Cat 25
　Places to Purchase your Tonkinese Cat Breed 26
　Cat Breeder Checklist 30

Physical and Behavioral Checklist for Tonkinese Cats 32
Acquiring and Adopting Tonkinese Cats.......................... 34
How About Adoption?... 34

Chapter Four: Housing and Accessories for Your Tonkinese Cats.. 39
Cat Keeping Must Have's! 40
Cat – Proofing Tips 43

Chapter Five: Essential Nutrients for Your Cat................... 49
Satisfying Your Tonkinese Needs.. 50
Feeding Guidelines for your Tonkinese Cat Breed 51
Types of Commercial Cat Foods... 53
Tips in Feeding Your Tonkinese Cat................................... 54
How to Feed Tonkinese Kittens? 55
How to Feed Adult/ Matured Tonkinese Cats?............. 55

Chapter Six: Housebreaking and Grooming Tips 57
Training Your Tonkinese Cat 58
Hygiene for Your Tonkinese Cat 62

Chapter Seven: Showing Your Tonkinese Cats 67
Cat Fanciers' Association (CFA) Score board 68
Showing Tips 73

Chapter Eight: Reproduction in Cats 77
Breeding Basics... 78

Signs of Copulation in Cats 79

Rearing Kittens 85

Chapter Nine: Common Illnesses of Tonkinese Cats 87

Common Health Problems 88

Vomiting 88

Feline Lower Urinary Tract Diseases (FLUTD) 89

Fleas 90

Tapeworms 91

Diarrhea 92

Eye Problems 92

Quick Summary and Care Sheet 95

Glossary of Cat Terms 101

Index 107

Photo Credits 111

References 113

Introduction

Tonkinese cats are personally known as a companion cat. Owners have easy time handling this breeds because it is a mix of a great house companion but also has an inquisitive mind. This breed is a sure pro for playing and inventing new games, one of which is playing fetch or a classic game of tag or even hide and seek, although Tonkinese kittens are naturally playful, but adults are still playful too.

Tonkinese will easily change your life, running your life and your home - but do not worry - they will not ruin your life! These cats would surely involve themselves with visitors and guest; they could be dubbed as your "door greeter" and would easily entertain your guests. However,

Introduction

you should not ignore or leave this breed alone - because they do not like to.

There are many things you need to learn about the Tonkinese cats. First time cat owners may be intimidated with these information - but you do not need to worry - because we will guide you every step of the way! We will be giving you general information, physical attributes, biological background of the Tonkinese cat. Aside from that, we will also guide you on how to take care of the Tonkinese cat, especially in terms of maintenance, grooming, health, nutrition, and habitat. You will also learn how to breed them, and how to show them.

We will be listing down the pros and cons of owning this pet, as well as different resource to help you understand this breed. We hope that you will learn a lot from this book, especially for those who are new in this field. There are many things to still learn. So, let's read on!

Chapter One: Biological and Historical Data

Choosing a new pet is an important family decision. You need to be committed in taking care of the pet not just at the beginning, but until the end. A cat is an excellent decision if you want to have a pet. Breeders usually make the kittens available between the ages of three to four months. However, kittens below the 12-week age should learn good behaviour from its family; learn socialization and skills needed for their new home. You could also teach them basic inoculations.

Taking care of a Tonkinese cat is very easy. This breed will think everyone is a friend and will not defend itself against danger. However, you still need to be armed with

Chapter One: Biological and Historical Data

additional knowledge to take care of your cat - as this is not an easy task.

In this section, we will give you the introduction about the Tonkinese cat. We will add its history and biological facts. You will know if the Tonkinese cat is fitted to you using this information, so you need to fully learn these things before you buy your first cat.

Taxonomy

Tonkinese cats have a scientific name of *Felis catus*. This breed belongs in Kingdom *Animalia*, Phylum *Chordata*, Class *Mammalia*, Order *Carnivora*, Family *Felidae*, Genus *Felis*, and Species *Domesticus*.

How Did Tonkinese Cats Came About?

Tonkinese cats are first cat breed to be ever recorderd in 1880. They are dubbed as the 'Chocolate Siamese.' It is widely acknowledged that the Burmese and Siamese cats are the parent breeds of the Tonkinese cat. However, the history of these three breeds is not that simple. The breeds are genetic cousins, their main difference lies between the colour of eyes and the coat colour; they were the same in shape

Chapter One: Biological and Historical Data

until the year 1970. The Tonkinese cat is created through a combination of solid coat pattern and color pointed pattern.

The breed has been bred in the West for a couple of years now. A writer, Harrison Weir, wrote that a cat that belonged to Hurbert Young, from Singapore, is a chocolate variety of the royal Siamese cat. This article was written in 1889. Weir pointed out that this cat is scared and beautiful.

Some people say that this breed is an excellent hybrid of the Siamese and Burmese cat. The American version of this breed is man-made but it has been in the west for quite some time now.

Dr. Robert Thompson imported Wong Mau, who became the matriarch of the Burmese. This happened in 1930. Wong Mau is noted to be the first Tonkinese.

Milan Greer, from New York, decided to crossbreed a Burmese and Siamese to really know if the offspring would be a Tonkinese. He mated a chocolate - pointed Siamese from Helen Arthur and Genevieve Gibson with his male Burmese. It resulted to five generations of Tonkinese cat.

In 1960, Margaret Conroy, a Canadian breeder, crossed a brown Burmese with a seal-point Siamese. She wanted to produce a cat that resembles the best traits of both breed. She was the one who wrote the breed standard for Tonkinese and also registered it to the Canadian Cat Association (CCA). Edith Lux changed the name from

Chapter One: Biological and Historical Data

Golden Siamese to Tonkinese. The name came from the Gulf of Tonkin, which is close to Burmese and Thai (Siamese) territories.

The Tonkinese cats area member of several cat organizations all over the world such as the Fédération Internationale Féline (FIFe), Cat Fanciers' Association (CFA), Australian Cat Federation (ACF), The International Cat Association (TICA), Canadian Cat Association (CCA – AFC), and many others.

Biological Facts

The Tonkinese cat is a muscular, medium sized cat that is heavier than it looks like. It weighs around 6 to 12 pounds for both female and male. It lives up to 13 or more years depending on how much you take care of it. It stands around 8 to 10 inches.

Males are noble and large, whereas the females are exquisitely feminine and smaller. Both of the sexes have almond shaped eyes which comes in sapphire, topaz, or sparkling aquamarine which matches their coat pattern, they also have a silky-short fur coat. They have a firm and strong body that match their slender legs.

The Tonkinese is noted to have many coat color variations such as medium brown, blue, platinum and, champagne (a paler shade of buff-beige). While European

Chapter One: Biological and Historical Data

standards accept fawn, tortoiseshell, cinnamon, red, caramel, cream, and apricot.

Tonkinese cats have shapely, well - spaced ears which are pricked forward and balanced perfectly on their sculptured head with gentle slopes and rounded edges. If you view the Tonkinese from the front, you could see an equilateral triangle.

Quick Facts

Origin: United States of America, Canada, Thailand

Pedigree: crossbreed of Siamese and Burmese

Breed Size: medium – size breed

Body Type and Appearance: Has a firm

Group: Cat Fanciers' Association (CFA), Fédération Internationale Féline (FIFe), The International Cat Association (TICA), Australian Cat Federation (ACF), Canadian Cat Association (CCA – AFC).

Height: 8 to 10 inches

Weight: average of 6 – 12 pounds

Coat Length: short ticked coat

Coat Texture: fine, silky, smooth, and soft

Chapter One: Biological and Historical Data

Color: brown, blue, platinum and, champagne (a paler shade of buff-beige). While European standards accept fawn, tortoiseshell, cinnamon, red, caramel, cream, and apricot.

Temperament: friendly, active, loving, demands attention, affectionate, involved in all activities, and likes to meet people

Strangers: friendly around strangers

Other Cats: if properly trained, introduced and socialized, they are generally good

Other Pets: friendly with other pets

Training: very trainable, clever, and responsive

Exercise Needs: does not need any special exercise, likes to play with toys and games

Health Conditions: generally healthy but could contract gingivitis, feline inflammatory bowel disease, excessive protein in body organs, upper respiratory infection, and etc.

Lifespan: average 10 to 16 years

These are just some basic information that you need to know about the Tonkinese cat. There are still a lot of things to learn. Let's read on and continue our journey!

Chapter Two: Keeping Tonkinese Cats

We have learned the breed's general information, as well as its history, physical attributes. We have known that this cat is a mixture of Siamese and Burmese, but now, we have to figure out if this breed is truly fitted for you and/or your family. Here, we will give you more information about the advantages and disadvantages of owning a Tonkinese cat. Aside from that, we will list down some legal requirements in keeping them as pets. Furthermore, we will also tackle its personality and behaviour with other pets and dogs, and the characteristics on why it is a great pet to own.

Chapter Two: Keeping Tonkinese Cats
Behavior, Characteristics, and Temperament

If you want to have Tonkinese as your own pet, you need to know its personality and attribute. You need to figure out if the cat's personality is a perfect match for you, especially if it likes company or now. In this section, we will give you information on its behaviour, characteristics, and temperament. Also, we will be talking about the cost of owning one, moreover, how to introduce or socialize this cat to other pet and cats.

Tonkinese cat is demanding yet affectionate. It knows that it wants to be on your lap and shoulder to carefully watch everything that you do, as well as the people around you. If your shoulder or lap isn't available, it would find the highest spot it can reach - making sure that it could see everything happening on the floor. Otherwise, you can also see it going through the pantry where its treats are stored.

Other than that, we can say that the Tonkinese cat is sociable and smart. It likes to answer the door and mingle with your guests; they like to shower their affection to the guests. They love to play hide and seek, tag, and fetch to anyone in the room!

If you are working, it is advisable to purchase two Tonkinese cats. Tonkinese cats become bored easily and love attention. If you already have two, they can keep each other company. A lone Tonkinese cat may cause trouble in your living room.

Aside from the aforementioned traits above, Tonkinese cats are highly intelligent. You need to challenge their brains in order to keep them interested in life. You can do this through tricks and puzzles toys, but you should reward them with kibbles or treats. Also, you can train them through positive reinforcement and persuasion. A Tonkinese is also talkative; although its voice isn't that loud and raspy like its Siamese ancestor.

Socializing with Children and Other Pets

Tonkinese cats are active and social, because of this, this breed is perfect for families especially with children, other than that they are also great with cat-friendly dogs. This breed plays fetch very well just like any dog, aside from that, it can learn tricks easily and loves the attention it will get from children, especially those who treats it politely and with utmost respect. It can live peacefully with any dog and cat, just to those who respect its authority. You must remember to guide and guard your pet when introducing it to a new environment; this is to ensure that they will get along together just fine.

Chapter Two: Keeping Tonkinese Cats

Is this the Right Breed for You?

Advantages:

- Tonkinese cats are a strong and healthy breed, because they are a crossbreed, they have few known illnesses.

- They are very affectionate and hungry for love from their owners.

- They are naturally curious, they want to know everything around them, so they stay on their owner's shoulder or the highest place they can reach.

- They get along well with other pets.

- They are loyal to their owners as well as their families.

- Tonkinese cats only need little grooming and upkeep.

- They are very intelligent, they like to be trained but they can teach themselves to play fetch.

- These cats are easily adaptable with other kids and pets.

- They require little exercise and tend to be indoors or in an enclosed space.

Disadvantages:

- They are known to be mischievous; they decide when to play and would never surrender until they play.

- They do not like to be left alone or have little attention for them. Make sure your Tonkinese has a companion if you need to leave.

- Tonkinese cats may have a tendency to be dominant, and even bully your other pet. You should supervise your cat if you are just introducing it to the family.

Cat Permits and Regulations

If you want to have your own Tonkinese cat, there are certain rules and regulations that you need to follow. This will ensure that you can travel inside and outside of your home country. However, licensing requirements for cats will vary on the country, state, and region.

The United States of America does not have any federal requirements for licensing your pets. However, these rules are regulated in their state level. Even though most states won't require you to license your pets, it is till best to license your pet - this is a good protection for both you and your pet.

In this portion, we will give you the guidelines in acquiring a license for your Tonkinese cat for both in the United States and the United Kingdom.

Licensing for Cats in the U.S.

You will need to spend around $10 or more for your cat's annual license, although the price will vary in the state that you live in. There is a discount for cat licenses for senior citizens; you only need to pay $5. So, you should let your grandparents license your cats for you.

After you have acquired your cat license, you will be given a number which can be linked to your contact details. If, unfortunately, your cat will get lost, the license can be used to track you down and return your pet to you. However, the information is only available if your cat is wearing a collar with an ID tag.

Even though your Tonk never leaves your house, it is still best to license it. This breed is very intelligent, and you might not know, it could outsmart you and it could be outside.

Chapter Two: Keeping Tonkinese Cats

An unfortunate disaster may lead your pet outside your home. If your cat is licensed, you can easily find your pet if s/he gets lost.

If you will apply for a cat license, it is best to search your municipal's or state government's website. You will see all the information about licensing. Other than that, you can easily download the application form to follow the correct procedure. Just fill out the form and pay the necessary fee. Some states do not require a fee, so you must see and check first how many its costs before paying the fee.

You may still need to provide necessary documentary requirement before getting your cat licensed. The documents are spayed and neuter proof, microchip, and current rabies certificate. Prepare these documents immediately so you will not have a hard time getting your pet licensed.

The aforementioned documents are the main documents needed in most states. However, you may still need to provide additional requirements in other places. A temporary license will be given to if you have not provided the necessary requirements in your area.

Some owners do not want to put a collar on their pets, if you are one of these people, you can have your cat micro-chipped. This microchip will serve the same function as the license, although this will be embedded under its skin so it will not be lost. Micro - chipping is a very quick and painless procedure for your cat, better have one today.

Chapter Two: Keeping Tonkinese Cats

Licensing for Cats in the U.K.

You do not need any licensing requirements in the United Kingdom, however, you need to have a special permit if you wish to travel with your cat whether inside or outside of the country.

There is a safety precaution before flying; you need to have your pet quarantined to make sure that it is not carrying any harmful disease just like rabies. Although rabies has been eradicated in the United Kingdom, it is still best to do the quarantine to maintain the rabies-free status.

Travel Permits for Cats

If you want to travel with your cat in countries other than the U.K. and U.S., you may need to provide the needed documents during your travel. The documents include the special permit for the cat, vaccination or rabies certificate, and certification of the current health condition that will ensure that your cat will not transfer any disease or virus outside the country. Other than that, there are other requirements you may need to provide according to the country where you want to visit, you may need to check their laws in bringing a pet to their country.

Chapter Two: Keeping Tonkinese Cats

Financial Aspects of Cat Keeping

In this part, we will give you an insight on how much you may need if you want to own a cat. There are a lot of expenses that you will experience, such as treats and food, cleaning and grooming supplies, vet care, toys, and other incidental costs you may encounter in the near future.

Having pets could be really costly, even though cat expenses are quite lower than any other pets, you still need to provide its basic necessities to provide and maintain a healthy and happy lifestyle and a sustainable environment for your pet.

These expenses will definitely hike up your daily budget, and the price will still vary depending on the place where you will be buying, the brand, nutrients in the food, and etc. If you really want to own a Tonkinese cat, you need to provide the necessary things for your pet. The first expenses you will have are the following: bed, toys, accessories, micro-chipping, initial vaccination, licensing, grooming supplies, spay/neutering, and etc. You might be surprise at the prices of these things, so you need to be very ready.

Chapter Two: Keeping Tonkinese Cats

Average Price of the Tonkinese Cats

The price of a Tonkinese cat heavily depends on where you will buy the cat. Also, other factor that may influence the price is the quality, pattern, breeder, color, bloodline, and geographic location of the cat. Usually, the price is from $300 to $1000.

However, some breeder might sell their cat for more than $1000, especially for those show quality. Fully vaccinated, vet-updated records and micro - chipped kitten's price may start at $400.

You need to remember this price range when buying your Tonkinese cat. Do not be fooled, especially when the price is too high or too low in the given price range.

Cat Accessories

There are also other things you need to buy when you purchase a Tonkinese cat. These things are toys, beds, food supplies, dishes, and grooming supplies. Also, you need to allot additional money for the following expenses: spaying/neutering procedure, micro-chipping, license renewal, vet consultation, and other needed items especially if you want to enter your cat in shows.

Chapter Two: Keeping Tonkinese Cats

Tonkinese cats are medium-sized cats, you will need to provide a normal sized to large sized bed for your cat. A large cat bed will keep your cat be comfortable especially if it goes bigger. The average cost of a cat bed is around $50 - $70. Aside from purchasing a cat bed for your Tonkinese cat, you will also need to provide high quality food, water bowls, dishes, and etc.

For your cat's food and water bowl, you need to purchase a food bowl made of stainless steel because it is very easy to clean, it cannot be eaten, played, or chewed on, at it does not acquire bacteria easily. You can also purchase a ceramic food and water bowl. You may need to spend around $30 for a quality set of stainless steel bowls.

Tonkinese cats are naturally playful, active, and curious. You need to provide them with a lot stimulation exercises that will keep their intelligence and curiousness occupied. You need to buy a lot of toys for your cats until you can figure out what it really likes. The minimum amount you may need to spend is around $20, the cost varies on the brand that you will be buying.

You need to provide great food to your Tonkinese cat for it to have a healthy diet that is an important factor to its wellness and health, especially that Tonkinese is a very active cat breed.

Chapter Two: Keeping Tonkinese Cats

Feeds for a high-quality diet, especially for medium sized cats, are not cheap. You need to find the feed that contains the right amount of nutrients that will maintain its healthy looking skin and disposition. You should allot around $50 for high quality cat foot which can last throughout the month. Also, you need to add an additional $10 for treats that will be used during your training session.

There will be times that you may need to walk your Tonkinese cat, although this breed is generally known as an indoor cat, you may need to let your cat walk or even present it in a show. In this scenario, you need to purchase several cat accessories, such as a leash and dresses, cat costumes, grooming supplies, and shelter repairs for the cat. You may need to spend around $50 on these accessories. However, the price still depends on the quality and brand of the product. Other than that, you may need to allot additional budget for extra costs such as replacement for toys, license renewal, and cleaning products.

Veterinary Expenses

As we have talked about earlier, kittens are more prone to contract bacterial and viral infection. You really need to take them to the vet for a check-up every six months or even every month.

Chapter Two: Keeping Tonkinese Cats

If you really want to keep your cat healthy, you should follow your vet's instruction on how to properly take care of your pet. However, you might need to take your cat often on the first year of its life - to receive the necessary vaccines and boosters it needs.

You may also need to allot additional money for micro-chipping, spaying/neutering surgery, vet consultations, and the initial vaccination for your kitten. These should be considered as an initial part of your budget because this will greatly affect your cat's health. There is no state or federal requirement stating that you need to have your cat micro-chipped in the United States and United Kingdom. Nonetheless, you still need to have your cat micro-chipped at an early stage of its life. As we have mentioned before, your Tonk could wander outside without you noticing, without a chip, you can never retrieve your cat easily.

If someone found your cat without any identification, they can take it to the shelter to have it scanned. The microchip will carry an identification number that is connected to your contact number. This chip is implanted under your cat's skin, the procedure only cost around $50, and typically is painless and very quick. However, you may need to provide certain documents to your local government to have your cat licensed.

Chapter Two: Keeping Tonkinese Cats

If you purchased or got your pet as a kitten, or during the early years of its life, you are required to have the kitten vaccinated. If you have purchased your kitten from a responsible breeder, s/he might have had the kitten vaccinated already, but, you still need to provide more vaccines and booster shots over the next couple of months and each year.

Tonks, especially when they are still kittens, are prone to common bacterial and viral infections. Aside from that, there are certain emergencies that may arise, so you may need to be safe and provide necessary vaccinations to prevent common illnesses such as Panleukopenia, Calicivirus, Rabies, Rhinotracheitis, and etc.

Other than that, you may need to provide the necessary boosters at an early age. Boosters can definitely help in lengthening the life span of your kitten. Boosters may cost around $50 or even more.

Other Medical Procedures

Other medical procedure includes spaying or neutering your pet. This procedure removes the reproductive system of your pet to prevent unwanted pregnancies. Aside from that, spaying or neutering can decrease the instance of having or contracting certain types of cancers as well as eliminating the possibility of having

Chapter Two: Keeping Tonkinese Cats

unwanted offspring.

The cost for spaying and neutering will heavily depend on where you will have it done and the gender of your cat. You need to bring your pet to a traditional veterinary surgeon, although the cost of spaying or neutering may be high, you can be assured that your surgeon could do the job easily and quickly. The cost of the spaying surgery is around $100 to $200, while the neutering surgery is around $50-$100.

The vet visits may cost around $40. Aside from this expense, you may still need to set aside another fund or budget for medical needs that will come up in the future. These are just some of the expenses that you will face if you want to own your own Tonk. If you are ready to face these expenses, let us continue our journey and read more.

Chapter Two: Keeping Tonkinese Cats

Chapter Three: Selecting the Right Tonkinese Cat

In this part, we will give you the criteria in finding the best and healthiest Tonkinese cat breed. Aside from that, we will help you find a trustworthy and reputable breeder in your area. We will also be helping you find the best place to purchase the Tonkinese cat. Moreover, we will be giving you links if ever want to buy your Tonkinese cat online, if you want to find a breeder, or even find rescue websites. These links will also give you more information about the Tonkinese cat. Before buying your Tonkinese cat, you need to consider the breeder and how he or she takes care of the pet, and if the cats are still kittens. Finding the reputable could be quite difficult, so we will help you find the best one out there.

Chapter Three: Selecting the Right Tonkinese Cat

Places to Purchase your Tonkinese Cat Breed

There are a lot of options in where you want to purchase your Tonkinese cat. In this section, we will help you decide where you want to buy your cat. We will be giving you the pros and cons of each place or choice. You must decide where you want to buy your Tonkinese cat.

Pet Stores

Local pet store is the first choice of everyone. People think that these pet stores have everything. However, this is not true. Here are the advantages and disadvantages of buying your Tonkinese cat from a local pet store.

Advantages:

✓ Pet stores are locally available in many areas.

✓ You can easily negotiate with the pet store.

✓ Some pet stores may even deliver your cat at home.

✓ This is one of the best options for busy people, because you just need to visit one area.

Chapter Three: Selecting the Right Tonkinese Cat

Disadvantages:

- ✓ Some pet shops might not have Tonkinese cats.
- ✓ You do not really know where the breed comes from.
- ✓ You can't ask the employees the history of the pet that they are selling.
- ✓ Some stores do not really take care of the cats well.

These are just some advantages and disadvantages of buying your Tonkinese cat breed from local pet stores. You may choose this option if you do not have enough time to go outside and talk to a lot of breeders.

Cat Hobbyists

Another great option that you have is through a cat hobbyist or a private breeder. In this scenario, you may need to find a referral through your friends or family. You can easily figure out if they are truly reputable or not. Here are other advantages and disadvantages of purchasing your cat from backyard or private breeders:

Advantages:

- ✓ You can personally meet the breeder and ask a lot of questions.

Chapter Three: Selecting the Right Tonkinese Cat

- ✓ You can know and see the parents' of the kitten you want to purchase.

- ✓ You can personally inspect if the breeder is taking care of the kitten properly.

- ✓ You can bargain the price of the kitten with the breeder.

- ✓ The breeder can give you a lot of information and s/he can help you in raising up your own cat.

Disadvantages:

- ✓ You may need to personally visit the breeder's house.

- ✓ You need to pick up the pet yourself

- ✓ You may need to talk to a lot of breeders to personally know and inspect the kitten you want to buy.

- ✓ You need to allot a lot of travel time and money to figure out if the breeder is reputable or not.

    This choice is best for people who want to talk to a lot of people and get to know a lot about their pet. If you plan to do this option, you will learn a lot about Tonks and you will be really exhausted.

Chapter Three: Selecting the Right Tonkinese Cat

Online Breeders/ Online Pet Shops

In today's era, online selling is another way of buying a cat.

Advantages:

- ✓ There are a lot of website where you can see and buy your own Tonk.
- ✓ This is best for people who are working and do not have a lot of time in finding the pet.

Disadvantages:

- ✓ You cannot really know if you have purchased a healthy breed.
- ✓ You can't personally check how the breeder has raised the kittens.

There are many risks in choosing this option; however, you can also join a lot of online forums to know the legitimate website and breeders in the internet.

Chapter Three: Selecting the Right Tonkinese Cat

Pet Conferences

Another great option is buying through pet conferences or cat conventions in your area. This is a great opportunity to meet and interact with cat owners and enthusiasts. Other than that, you can personally critique the breeders and their litters. You can be assured of the quality as well as the papers and licensing requirements. Also, you can meet other pet owners and breeders from this.

Cat Breeder Checklist

You have already known where you can buy your first cat; it is now time to know the traits that make a reputable breeder. You need to first select the breeder before you but the pet. You need to find the breeder that is caring, responsible, reputable, and the one who you think can interact and breeds the cat well. Here are some traits and guidelines you need to find in a responsible cat breeder:

- Look for key information and history about the breeder if they have website.

- If the website is vague or does not provide enough information, do not waste your time and look for another breeder again.

Chapter Three: Selecting the Right Tonkinese Cat

- Check licenses and registrations at TICA or CFA, if they ever registered in one.

- Ask for the registration number, health information, and the breeding stock about the cat or litter that they raising.

- A reputable breeder will also ask you a lot of questions about yourself. The breeder would want to make sure that his/her cat would go to great homes.

- You can also ask the breeder questions about his experience in breeding and taking care of Tonks. A reputable breeder can answer any question you have.

- Tour the facility in which the breeder keeps his or her litter, you can see if the kittens are well kept.

- If the facility is unorganized or unclean, you should not purchase your kitten from him or her.

- You need to see that the litter is in good condition and all of them are active and healthy looking.

- If even one of the litters is sick, look for another breeder as diseases can easily pass through different kittens.

Chapter Three: Selecting the Right Tonkinese Cat
Physical and Behavioral Checklist for Tonkinese Cats

After knowing where and who to buy from, you need to buy your very own Tonk! You can either purchase a cat or a kitten - it is totally up to your preference. You have now chosen the responsible and reputable breeders, you just need now to make sure that the Tonk kitten is healthy not only behaviourally but also physically, aside from that, you need to make sure that the cat matches your personality.

Here are the attributes you need to look for when purchasing a healthy Tonkinese cat breed:

- Look and examine the kitten's or cat's body for signs of injuries, illnesses, or any imperfection.

- Check coat and skin colour

- Check to see if the cat or kitten has complete body parts

- The pet should have bright, clear eyes with no discharge

- You should see that the kitten's or cat's ears are clean and clear, with no visible signs of inflammation or discharge.

Chapter Three: Selecting the Right Tonkinese Cat

- There should not be a swollen or distended stomach for your cat or kitten

- The kitten or cat should be able to run and walk properly and normally without any problems.

- Also check the mouth, make sure that the gums and teeth are in excellent condition

- Do not choose the cats that look lethargic or those who have difficulty in moving because they could be sick.

- Your chosen kitten must be playful, active, and interacting with other members of the litter in a healthy and happy manner.

- Observe the whole litter; you need to see how the cats or kittens interact with one another, so you can know their individual personalities.

- Try to interact with the pets, try to see if they react wildly or calmly to your touch or while playing.

- Try to pick each one of the litter to figure out if they are frightened of human touch, if they are scared, this could mean that the cat is not properly socialized yet.

Chapter Three: Selecting the Right Tonkinese Cat

- If you can see that the whole group is in good condition, then you can be sure that the breeder is truly reputable. It is now time to choose the best kitten or cat that connects with you.

Acquiring and Adopting Tonkinese Cats

There are a lot of Tonkinese breeders everywhere. You really need to do some extensive research to decide which breeder you can buy your kitten or cat from. If you decide to buy a kitten, you can find the best breed from a local breeder. However, you can still choose to adopt an adult cat. Many adult cats are abandoned and left alone by their previous owners, and these cats are looking for a new home.

How About Adoption?

Adopting an adult cat can also have its perks, some shelters give away accessories and cages for the cat. Other than that, adult cats are already vaccinated with complete boosters, also, they have also been neutered or spayed, litter - trained, and well socialized. Adopting an adult cat does not only mean saving a life, it is also economical. Here are some breeders and rescue websites in the United States and United Kingdom:

Chapter Three: Selecting the Right Tonkinese Cat

United States Breeders and Rescue Websites

Tonkinese Cats and More

<http://www.tonkinese.me/rescue-and-re-homing.html>

Kittens, Adopt Adult, Rescue, Tonkinese Breeders

<http://www.tonkinesebreedassociation.org/Referrals.htm>

Tonkinese Rescue

<http://tonkinese.rescueme.org/>

Tonkinese Breed Club

<http://www.tonkinese.info/rescue---re-homing-lost--found.html>

Tonkinese Cat Rescue Group Directory

<http://tonkinese.rescueshelter.com/>

Rameses Tonkinese

<http://www.ramesescats.co.uk/rescue/>

Chapter Three: Selecting the Right Tonkinese Cat

Pet Guardian Angels of America

<http://pgaa.com/tonkinese/>

Pendragon Tonkinese

<http://www.pendragontonks.com/>

Titantonks Tonkinese Cats

<http://www.titantonks.co.uk/>

All About Dogs and Cats: Resource Center for Canine and Feline Lovers

<http://www.allaboutdogsandcats.com/Cats/PurebredCatRescue.html>

Anniesong Tonkinese

<https://www.anniesongtonkinese.com/page/buying-a-tonkinese/#/page/buying-a-tonkinese/>

Tails

<http://www.tailsinc.com/resources/boston-cat-breed-rescue-groups/>

Chapter Three: Selecting the Right Tonkinese Cat

Tonkinese Cat Rescue

<http://tonkinesebreedassociation.org/>

Amimao Tonkinese

<http://www.amimao.us/>

United Kingdom Breeders and Rescue Websites

Strawberry Persian + Pedigree Cat Rescue UK

<http://strawberrypersianpedigreecatrescue.co.uk/>

Tonkinese Cat Club

<https://www.tonkinesecatclub.co.uk/>

Kittens for Adoption

<http://www.kittensforadoption.co.uk/catclassifieds/search/cat-breeds:tonkinese-cat>

Chorus Tonkinese Cats

<http://www.choruscats.uk/>

Titantonks Tonkinese Cats

<http://www.titantonks.co.uk/>

Chapter Three: Selecting the Right Tonkinese Cat

Time for Paws
<http://www.timeforpaws.co.uk/blog/tonkinese-cat-owners-guide/>

Purebreds Plus Cat Rescue
<http://purebredsplus.org/>

Pets4Home
<https://www.pets4homes.co.uk/sale/cats/tonkinese/>

Tonkinese Kittens
<http://www.tonkinesekitten.co.uk/>

Kitten List
<http://www.kittenlist.co.uk/breeders/search.php?cp=2&bt=369>

Tonkyway and Sialaxy by Julie Singleton
<http://www.tonkyway.co.uk/>

Hylily Tonkinese & Samburu Sokokes
<http://www.hylily-tonkinese.co.uk/>

These are just some of the rescue and breeder sites that may help you gather a whole lot of information about you cat. Make sure that you read them one by one to gain more knowledge about your beloved pet.

Chapter Four: Housing and Accessories for Your Tonkinese Cats

You have already bought your Tonkinese cat; you now need to learn its proper maintenance, setting up a suitable environment so it can grow happily and healthily with you and your family. In this chapter, we will give you the basics in your cat's habitat requirement such as its accessories and shelter. We will also be giving you cat proofing techniques before you welcome your cat or kitten in your home. Also, we will be giving you guidelines in maintaining an adequate living space for the cat/s.

Chapter Four: Housing and Accessories for Your Tonkinese Cat Keeping Must Have's!

Just like any other cats, your Tonkinese cat will need enough space to walk, other than that; it needs a cat bed for it to relax to after a long day of games and fun.

You need to buy a cat bed that will be big enough to your cat or kitten. You may buy the biggest bed so your cat will be very comfortable and also economic, because your cat will use it for a long time and you do not need to buy a bigger bed in the near future. Other than that, you can add bed sheets or even a pillow for added comfort. However, you may need to buy a disposal pillow because your cat may easily play and destroy with it.

Some owners say that some cats may want to sleep on the floor, or a box, or anywhere that is comfortable to them. If this is the case, you do not force your cat to sleep on the new bed that you had bought it, especially if it is new to your home, or new as a cat owner. Your cat may still be adjusting to the environment you have made for him or her. You can sprinkle catnip to the bed to encourage the cat to sleep in the bed. You may even put several beds in different places so it can 'pick' a spot where it wants to spends the time the most.

Some owners prefer buying a cage for their Tonks, just like the bed, you may need to buy a big cage so you will not have to buy another cage every time the cat grows

Chapter Four: Housing and Accessories for Your Tonkinese

larger. However, your Tonk will not like to stay in that cage because it prefers being with their humans and having all the attention it can get. The cage may be necessary if you have other pets present in your house as they may fight and not socialize properly.

You need to provide an exercise pen inside your house if you do not want your cat to run loose, this is different from the cat bed or cage. Tonkinese cats are naturally curious yet active, they would like run and roam around their house, however you do not want them to roam around freely or even taste and sniff everything inside the house. In this scene, you need to give them their own space that includes a lot of toys and stuff that will capture their attention and revert their mind off of your appliances, supplies, or even your figurines.

Other than that, you need to provide a cat tree or perch because cats love to climb anything that they can see. A good alternative is placing shelves on your wall, this will give your cat a place to perch on, it will still give your cat a chance to look at the whole place and feel secured. Be careful in putting up decorations in your house, especially those that can be easily knocked over by your cat, cats really love knocking off things on shelves as a game.

Aside from having cat bed or perch, you may also need to provide a lot of engaging and stimulating toys to play and put off excess energy. Tonks are naturally active

Chapter Four: Housing and Accessories for Your Tonkinese

that is why they need as much exercise and play time they need. This task will help your Tonk be physically and mentally stimulated. You can also play with your pet; it will serve as your bonding moment as it is both fun and healthy for the both of you.

Cats can occupy themselves for long hours, so you will not need much expensive toys to keep them stimulated. However, you may need to still buy them toys to keep them active and fit.

Aside from buying your pet store-bought toys, you can also improvise or DIY its toys! You can use your regular household stuff to make your kitten or cat lively and active! You just need to be interactive and creative during play time such as golf balls, ping pong balls, empty cardboard boxes, flash lights, paper bags, dangling objects, and other usual objects. Before using these items, you may need to remove some parts that your cat or kitten may chew or swallow such as plastic bag, string, pins, needles, ribbons, feathers, rubber bands, paper clips, tinsels, or any other small decorations. For best scenario, you may need to supervise your cat or kitten when playing to keep your cat out of danger.

Chapter Four: Housing and Accessories for Your Tonkinese Cat – Proofing Tips

If you have not bought your cat yet, there is still time to prepare yourself and your home. You need to do this task to protect your cat from various household hazards and prevent unwanted situations or accidents. In this section, we will give you some guidelines on how to cat - proof your home:

Proof Tip #1: Remove possible poisonous plants.

- Cats like to chew on plants and grass, some of these may be dangerous, irritating, and even deadly to your pet. Even your usual plants could cause diarrhea and vomiting. You should not plant these plants or keep them out of reach. If your cat likes green things to play with, you can purchase cat grass, just to be safe.

Proof Tip #2: Keep away the cleaning supplies.

- Child proof latches are not only used for children. You can also use these latches to keep your cat away from eating, licking, and even your cleaning products. Other than that, cleaning products contain dangerous chemicals that could kill your cat. Also you do not want your cat to be playing with your precious pots

Chapter Four: Housing and Accessories for Your Tonkinese

and pans.

Proof Tip #3: Keep your medicine/s away

- You should keep all the medicines, both the prescription and over-the-counter - for both animals and humans, in a secure cabinet. Make sure that you will not drop any pills on the floors - this could be deadly to your pet.

Proof Tip #4: Stow your breakables

- Keep your breakables away from your cat. Your cat love going everywhere! They would jump on sideboards, cabinets, tables, and even bookshelves. They can break and knock over fragile items, and play and run with fragile broken pieces.

Proof Tip #5: Unplug your electronics

- Unplug all electrical cords especially when you are not using them. Cats love to chew and they could be electrocuted if you have not unplugged your cords. You need to put your cords in a cord protector to prevent your cat from ever chewing it again. You can also put hot sauce to the cords to stop your cat from ever licking and chewing it.

Chapter Four: Housing and Accessories for Your Tonkinese

Proof Tip #6: Tie up everything!

- o Keep the blind cords and even the draperies out of reach. Your cat could play, chew, but even strangle itself on the cord. It could lead them to getting wounded or even choking.

Proof Tip #7: Check all the places your cat can potentially hide

- o Look inside the dryer before closing the door, and keep it closed when not in use. Cats love to hole up in dark, quiet places, which can be a recipe for a tragedy. Kittens often climb into refrigerators, freezers and dresser drawers, so check these, too, before closing them.

Proof Tip #8: Remove everything on your table

- o Do not use the tablecloths from your table unless your will be using it. Kittens love to see and be curious about what is happening at your table and try to climb up from there. It could result to broken things, but some might result to injury.

Chapter Four: Housing and Accessories for Your Tonkinese
Proof Tip #9: Put a lid on the toilet

- Keep your seats down. You cat can fall in and not get out.

Proof Tip #10: Make sure you have screens

- Buy screen doors and windows that have sturdy, secure latches. You do not want your cat to slip out unnoticed.

- Have padded perches indoors beside a window frame or in your patio so that your pet could ehang out and enjoy. However, you should not leave your doors and screens unlocked because they may still slip out unnoticed.

Proof Tip #11: Keep your cat busy!

- Train your cat to walk on leash when you go out.

- Buy a cat tree so your cat can climb and play inside your house.

- Buy enough toys for your cat to play with. This is to prevent any incidents involving your furniture or decorations.

Chapter Four: Housing and Accessories for Your Tonkinese

These are just things to remember especially when keeping your cat at home. Make sure you prepare your cat on time before taking it home; this is to prevent incidents and tragedies.

Chapter Four: Housing and Accessories for Your Tonkinese

Chapter Five: Essential Nutrients for Your Cat

Giving healthy food will surely help your Tonkinese cat be healthy and happy. You should consider the level of activity, weight, and age when feeding your Tonkinese cat. This is to ensure that your cat will meet the nutritional needs. Just like everyone, your cat should be given the recommended and correct amount of food for balanced nutrition. A proper diet could help your cat have longer life and protect them from various diseases and illnesses.

In this chapter, we will give you the nutritional needs, feeding guidelines, foods to avoid, and some of the best cat food for your Tonkinese cat. Even if you are a pro in taking care of a cat, you should take note of these things because Tonkinese cats have special and specific needs.

Chapter Five: Essential Nutrients for Your Cat

What Does My Tonk Eat?

Just like any other cats, your Tonkinese is highly carnivorous animal. You should keep in mind that they like to eat meat. You should give them food enriched with meat or they could be picky eaters in the future.

Tonkinese is a close relative of tigers, lions, and even leopards, you need to be aware that they they will not eat grass, apple, or even milk. You should not be surprised if your Tonk will not eat the food that you will give it, especially if it does not like it. Tonkinese is not like humans and dogs. They need fats and proteins. Never give your cat dog food as this may be fatal to your Tonk, because it will not meet the dietary needs because dog food contain high portions of carbohydrates, which the cat can never digest and never need. Carbohydrates can lead to weight gain and eventually diabetes.

Satisfying Your Tonkinese Needs

You need to make sure that the food that you will buy for your Tonkinese cat will satisfy the standards set by the American Association of Feed Control Officials (AAFCO). If the food that you will buy will be up for the standards, you can be assured that your Tonk will get the necessary and right nutrition needed.

Chapter Five: Essential Nutrients for Your Cat

Ignore the superficial terms such as 'best', 'premium' or even 'natural', which has no strict standard. You can also ask your doctor on what food he or she can recommend. You need to do a taste test to see if your cat truly enjoys the food and will not have any issues such as constipation. However, if your cat does not like the food, make sure to have other foods ready. If your Tonk stop eating, your Tonk could be in an extreme risk of liver failure or even death.

If you want to change the food that you will give, you need to replace the food in small quantities over a course of a week. This will enable your Tonk to accept the change and reduces the stomach discomfort your cat could have.

Feeding Guidelines for your Tonkinese Cat Breed

How much food do I need to give to my Tonkinese? There are a lot of things to consider before feeding your Tonk. Some things that could affect are the activity of your cat, sterilization surgery, and even weight. You can consult your vet, s/he will tell you how much you need to feed your cat and how often, this will ensure that you will hit your target and recommended weight.

When you have determined how much you will feed your cat, you need to stick to it. You need to train your Tonk to stick to how much you will feed it. You need to remember

Chapter Five: Essential Nutrients for Your Cat

that it is difficult to get rid of the excess weight once they are obese.

Aside from this, you need to schedule when you will feed your Tonk. Tonks like to eat in small portions during the day. You can also give half in the morning and half in the evening for portion control. Although you might be tempted to give snacks, keep it in a minimum, because your cat might be full and not get the recommended food requirements.

Free-feeding is a new trend wherein you leave food for your pet and it is up to them when to eat. Although this might be enticing, most vets and experts do not encourage you to try this trend, because cats are natural hunters, which mean they work hard for their food. It is unnatural for them to have available food 24/7. This choice is uneconomic and very dangerous for their health. Cats can only eat small meals at specific periods of time.

Cats can't really eat whenever they like, they only like to eat after playing or doing an activity. Having food available anytime will just mess with their nature and brain. Other than that, free-feeding could cause behavioural problems, if you practice free-feeding, your cat will relieve anywhere and anytime it wants - which is not really that sanitary. It is still best that you feed your cat in small amounts rather than free -feeding it.

Chapter Five: Essential Nutrients for Your Cat

Types of Commercial Cat Foods

There are a lot of cat foods available in the market. You just need to choose what you think the best for your cat. You have the choice to feed them: dry, semi moist and canned. Dry food contains six to 10% moisture, while semi moist has 15 - 30%, and canned at 75% moisture.

In general, canned food contains more protein, animal product, and fat, it also contains lesser carbohydrates than semi-moist and dry food. You must inspect the food labels, especially the percentage of fat, water, fibre, and protein in the food. You can ask your vet on how to read the food labels properly to get the best from the food that you will be giving.

For adult Tonks, you need to give them dry food because it contains more benefits for them. Dry food will prevent the cat from overeating that would lead to obesity. Other than that, it could help your cat have stronger teeth because of chewing. Some cat like wet food, so you can add a bit of wet food to the dry food to make it tastier and a little bit better.

Chapter Five: Essential Nutrients for Your Cat

Tips in Feeding Your Tonkinese Cat

You need to fully understand your Tonk to know how much it eats and how often it will eat. Other than that, you should be strict in feeding your cat; you need to train when you want to eat and how much it needs to eat.

Here are some guidelines in feeding your cat:

- ✓ You should have different spots or areas for feeding, litter box, and sleeping/resting area.

- ✓ If you own multiple cats, each should have its own water and food station. This place should have its own quiet place where your cat could spend time alone.

- ✓ The water bowls must be shallow and wide. You should change the water daily. Some cats want to drink from a water fountain or a dripping faucet.

- ✓ Some cats prefer to eat from shallow plates or plates. This is to prevent their whiskers from touching the sides.

- ✓ Separate the food and water bowls from each other.

- ✓ You should always keep your water and food dishes clean.

- ✓ Always maintain and measure the correct food allotment for your cat.

Chapter Five: Essential Nutrients for Your Cat

These are just some of the guidelines for you whenever you are feeding your cat. Make sure to follow these things to have your cat fully satisfied and happy whenever it is eating.

How to Feed Tonkinese Kittens?

Your kittens should eat more frequently. You should feed them in large quantities because they are growing, however, you must know that they have limited space in their tiny stomachs.

When your kitten is already at eight weeks, you should feed it around five meals a day. At the six month period, you need to decrease the food quantity to two meals a day because they are around 75% of their adult size.

You can change the kitten food to cat food at around eight to 10 months of age because their growth is complete at six months. Kittens and cats do not really need milk. At the age of 12 weeks, kittens become lactose intolerant, which means they cannot digest milk sugar. Too much milk could potentially lead to intestinal upset and diarrhea.

How to Feed Adult/ Matured Tonkinese Cats?

You should always give your cat high quality commercial adult cat food because it is formulated to have all the nutrients your cat should have. You can use either dry

Chapter Five: Essential Nutrients for Your Cat

or wet food, but you should always give it at correct amount or else you could overfeed your cat.

As we have mentioned earlier, when a cat becomes obese or overweight, it is very difficult to shed off the excess weight.

You can feed small meals of wet food once or twice a day and alternate it with dry food in between. This strategy is okay as long as your cat is receiving the correct number of calories and having his daily exercise.

You need to remember that each chat has its own diet and feeding behaviour, because it has its own unique needs and characteristics. The number of meals and its quantity will heavily depend on the individual preference and activity of your cat. You should feed your cat according to the stage he or she is into. Other than that, cats with certain illnesses or diseases need prescription diet that would delay or control the symptoms.

Choosing the best cat food is very difficult, there are many available brands that would brag that they are the best, but not all pet foods are equal. You need to determine which pet food has the best ingredients. Ask your vet to interpret the information and ask him or her the best diet to meet your cat's need. If you are having difficulties, is it still best to ask your vet for help.

Chapter Six: Housebreaking and Grooming Tips

After knowing a lot of things, you now need to learn how to train and groom your own Tonkinese cat. Tonkinese cats are naturally smart and curious. It wants to explore and understand the world it revolves in. In this essence, you should try to train your cat at an early age. In grooming, you will not have a lot of problem because Tonkinese cats do not shed a lot compared to other cats.

In this portion, we will give you tips and tricks in training your cat, other than that, you will also learn with grooming techniques, and some suggestions on how to keep them clean even through their most stubborn behaviour.

Chapter Six: Housebreaking and Grooming Tips

Training Your Tonkinese Cat

Just like any pet, training your Tonkinese cat breed is a very difficult yet beneficial and rewarding experience between you and your pet. Training your cat is a great chance of bonding and getting to know your pet. You need to train your pet to be well-behaved Tonk in the future. As we have repeatedly said, Tonks are very clever and smart, and they like knowing what happens to their environment as much as possible.

You need to create a solid connection and have a solid rapport with your pet. In this manner, you should establish the trust before you even train your cat.

Here are some things you might want to remember when you are training your cat:

Training Tip #1: Hand Signals
- o Set a standard hand signal for your pet. You can clap or even whistle because it is the easiest thing you can do.

Training Tip #2: Do not use other signaling devices
- o Avoid having bells or other devices when training. This might confuse your cat, other than that; you cannot use the device anymore when

Chapter Six: Housebreaking and Grooming Tips

there is an emergency.

Training Tip #3: Train When Hungry

- Make sure that your cat is hungry when training. You can give your cat some treats when training to him/her to follow your command easily.
- You need to repeat the exercise until your cat has already learned the command.

Training Tip #4: Teach different thing
- There are a lot of things to teach your cat, go and try it with your beloved pet.

Training Tip #5: Use treats
- You can use treats as positive reinforcement, especially when the cat has correctly followed and repeated the exercise.

Training Tip #6: Litter Train Your Cat
- It is very difficult to litter train your cat. You should repeatedly put your kitten in the box. He might do other things at first, but he is just getting accustomed to his new box. You may need to repeat the process over and over again to make your cat more comfortable.

Chapter Six: Housebreaking and Grooming Tips

Training Tip #7: "Rinse and Repeat"
- Litter training is a very difficult task. You may need to put your kitten in the box a few times every day until he gets used to it. Make sure that the place is quiet and easy to reach.

Training Tip #8: Separate Litter Box for Different Cats
- If you have more than one cat, make sure you give different litter boxes. Cats like to have their own space, so make sure he has them. You need to have one box plus an extra.

Training Tip #9: Choose a Suitable Litter Box
- You make sure that the litter box is suitable for your cat. You have plenty of options for your cat to choose from.

Training Tip #10: Always Clean Your Litter Box
- Do not let much dirt and litter pile up in the box, because it will definitely be unsanitary. Clean and scoop it frequently, this will also prevent your cat from eating its own poop.

Chapter Six: Housebreaking and Grooming Tips

Training Tip #11: Getting rid of the scratching behavior

- Cats really love to scratch things; however, you should not this behaviour completely. Scratching is pretty normal and is an important behaviour for the cats. It helps them to fully stretch their toes and spread their scents using the pads on their feet.

- If your cat is really persistent in scratching the furniture, you may need to buy a scratching post or pole in the house. The pole will help your cat use this instead of the furniture, just sprinkle with dried catnip or a liquid catnip spray. You can also give your cats treats when it is using the scratching post; this is to encourage him to continue using it.

Training Tip #12: Controlling loud behavior

- Cats sometimes like do demand attention because they do not want to be alone. Tonks are really affectionate and would want your full attention as possible. However, your Tonk might get too loud. To stop this behaviour, you should not give in too much to your cat.

- If he continues to meow for your attention, but you give it to him, you are reinforcing or 'okay-ing' the behaviour. Your cat would learn to surrender if it knows that play time is officially over.

Hygiene for Your Tonkinese Cat

Cat produces natural oils that will help its skin be moisturized. We groom cats not for keeping them clean but for maintaining and improving their skin condition. Cat grooming will help distribute natural body oils that will keep the cat's skin silky, soft, and healthy. Here are the things you need to remember when grooming your cat:

Grooming Tip #1: Regular grooming

- You should groom/bathe your cat once or twice a week or every other day. Your cat can get used to it and it will not be a major chore if you do groom/bathe him regularly.

Grooming Tip #2: Use a Tub

- Use a small tub or even your sink and fill it around one to inches or lukewarm water. The water will only be used to damp your cat's

Chapter Six: Housebreaking and Grooming Tips

skin. You should not fill the tub fully because your cat might drown or get sick.

Grooming Tip #3: Mild Shampoo

- Make sure you only use a mild, fragrance - free baby shampoo for your cat. Use the shampoo to massage your cat's skin using your hand or with a cloth.

Grooming Tip #4: Use a Soft Cloth

- After you have given your cat a bath, use a soft cloth and warm water to remove all the soap. If your cat is already used to taking a bath, you can use flowing water to rinse its back.

Grooming Tip #5: Make sure to regularly brush your cat's teeth

- Habitual brushing of your cat's teeth can decrease the chance of periodontal disease. Many pet owners often skip the dental hygiene, but this is a serious mistake. Brushing the cat's teeth is just easy, although you might need to buy a pet toothbrush and toothpaste to do it.

Chapter Six: Housebreaking and Grooming Tips

- You might need to repeat the tooth brushing over and over again to get your cat accustomed to it. You can brush you cat's teeth every day, but you can start doing it every few times a week.

Grooming Tip #6: Clip your cat's nails.

- Human nails are just like cat's nail. With this in mind, you should know that their nails need to be trimmed occasionally. You can trim your cat's nail once a week or even twice a month. But before you get that clipper, make sure that you get a help from your vet or a professional groomer to show you how.

Grooming Tip #7: Clean off their ears regularly

- Tonks have alert ears, so you should not worry about ear infections. These infections are only common to breeds that have folded ears; these ears limit the amount of air flow in the inner portion of the ear. Remember, wet ears are a great breeding ground for bacteria. However, you still need to clean your cat's ears just to remove the wax in it.

Chapter Six: Housebreaking and Grooming Tips

- To be able to clean its ears, you can use a cat ear cleaning solution and just put a few drops in the ear canal. Next, you massage the base of the cat's ear to distribute the solution, then wiping with a clean cotton ball.

Chapter Six: Housebreaking and Grooming Tips

Chapter Six: Housebreaking and Grooming Tips

Chapter Seven: Showing Your Tonkinese Cats

Tonkinese cats are very great for shows. If you want to let the world know how beautiful and great your cat it, you can enter it in shows! There are a lot of competitions and shows you can enter your Tonk to. Your cat has a lot of potential talent you can surely improve on. However, there are certain requirements for the breed you need to comply to. In this portion, we will discuss the breed standard for the Tonkinese cat, and some guidelines to help your cat in entering the show. This will help you if you really want to show your cat or not.

Chapter Six: Housebreaking and Grooming Tips

Cat Fanciers' Association (CFA) Score board

HEAD
- Profile — 8
- Muzzle and chin — 6
- Ears — 6
- Eye shape and set — 5

Total: 25

BODY
- Torso — 15
- Legs and feet — 5
- Tail — 5
- Muscle tone — 5

Total: 30

COAT — 10

Total: 30

COLOR
- Coat color — 25
- Eye color — 10

Total: 35

Chapter Six: Housebreaking and Grooming Tips

GENERAL BODY

- ✓ Intermediate Type
- ✓ Not cobby or svelte
- ✓ The cat should be alert and active, with great muscular development.
- ✓ The cat should be heavy.
- ✓ The breed should be balanced in size and proportion.

HEAD AND MUZZLE

- ✓ Slightly rounded wedge and somehow longer than it is wide, with high gently planed cheekbones.
- ✓ Blunt, long, and wide muzzle
- ✓ Slight gently curved whisker break, that follows the line in the wedge
- ✓ There is a slight stop at eye level.
- ✓ Gentle contour with a rise from the nose stop to the forehead.
- ✓ There is a slight convex curve to the forehead.

Chapter Six: Housebreaking and Grooming Tips

EARS

- ✓ Alert
- ✓ Medium in size.
- ✓ Oval tips
- ✓ broad at the base
- ✓ The hairs on the ears should be very short and close-lying.

EYES

- ✓ Open almond shape
- ✓ Slanted along the cheekbones up to the outer edge of the ear.
- ✓ It should be proportionate in size to the face.

EYE COLOR

- ✓ The eye colour should have depth, clarity, and brilliance of color preferred.
- ✓ The colour should be best seen in natural light.

Chapter Six: Housebreaking and Grooming Tips

BODY

- ✓ Medium length torso
- ✓ Your Tonk should be well-developed, with great muscular strength
- ✓ The body should be proportionate and balanced.
- ✓ Firm, taut, and well - muscled abdomen

LEGS and FEET

- ✓ Fairly slim
- ✓ Proportionate in length
- ✓ Hind legs should be slightly longer than front.
- ✓ Paws are more oval than round

Toes

- ✓ Five toes in front and four behind.

TAIL

- ✓ Proportionate in length to body

Chapter Six: Housebreaking and Grooming Tips

COAT

- ✓ Medium short in length
- ✓ Close-lying
- ✓ Fine
- ✓ Soft and silky
- ✓ Has a lustrous sheen.

BODY COLOR

- ✓ There is an allowance for lighter body especially in young cats
- ✓ Cats will get darken with age.

WITH PENALTY

- ✓ Extreme ranginess or cobbiness.
- ✓ Definite nose break.
- ✓ Round eyes.

DISQUALIFICATIONS

- ✓ Yellow eyes in mink colors.

Chapter Six: Housebreaking and Grooming Tips

- ✓ White locket or button.
- ✓ Crossed eyes.
- ✓ Tail faults.

Showing Tips

There are a lot of things to do before you can show your cat. Your cat needs to be a strong breed example for your cat to do great in a show. Also, make sure you read the rules and regulation of each show you want your Tonkinese cat to enter. Other than that, you need to make sure that your cat can meet all the qualification of the breed, because there are a lot of things you need to accomplish before the show. Below are some guidelines that you need to following when preparing your cat for a show:

- o **Showing Tip #1:** You need to present your cat's papers and license to make sure that your cat is properly classified that conforms to the rules of the show. Make sure that you have the necessary documents ready immediately.

Chapter Six: Housebreaking and Grooming Tips

- **Showing Tip #2:** Make sure to fill up the registration form correctly, provide all the necessary details, and submit the form on time.

- **Showing Tip #3:** Shows have entry fees. Make sure you are prepared to pay the fee in the show or competition you want to enter it.

- **Showing Tip #4:** Declaw your cat before the show. Declawed cats are allowed without any penalty.

- **Showing Tip #5:** Thoroughly make sure that your cat is registered to the show that you want it to compete to.

- **Showing Tip #6:** You need to follow the proper age bracket or category of the show you want to enter in. Some organizations can allow kittens to enter as young as three months, while some have specific restrictions.

- **Showing Tip #7:** Bring the necessary things for the show. Some shows can provide you with things, but most of the time, it is incomplete. Make sure you bring your gear before the show starts.

Chapter Six: Housebreaking and Grooming Tips

- **Showing Tip #8:** Bring food and water for both you and the cat. You will spend all day at the show or competition. Make sure both you and cat can last throughout the day.

- **Showing Tip #9:** Make sure you pay attention to everything happening in the show. Some shows give a list of things you need to provide before the main event begins. Some may even post it on their website or given directly to your email.

- **Showing Tip #10: Prepare the following items:**

    - Cage curtains and clips to hang them.
    - Needed necessary grooming supplies, such as nail clippers
    - Confirmation slip that you got at entry.
    - Cat litter and litter pan.
    - food/water bowls and food treats
    - proof of vaccinations and Veterinary records
    - Veterinary records and your cat's pedigree.
    - Extra food, clothes, and water for yourself.
    - Garbage bag for clean-up.
    - A bed or blanket for the cage.

Chapter Six: Housebreaking and Grooming Tips

These are the common things you need to know about showing your pets. It might be difficult at first, but the rewards you can reap from the show is very satisfying.

Chapter Eight: Reproduction in Cats

There comes a time when you want to breed and produce more Tonkinese cat, maybe it is time to take care more and raise more Tonkinese kittens. Who knows, you could be the next reputable breeder in your area someday! In this section, we will provide you with lots of information about your Tonkinese cat, such as sexual dimorphism, breeding process, the mating procedure, and the things you need to prepare when your kittens will be born.

Chapter Eight: Reproduction in Cats

Breeding Basics

Just like any mammals, Tonkinese cats are sexually dimorphic animals. This means that their sex/gender can be easily identified based on their physical traits or characteristics, as well as looking at its reproductive organs. There is also a difference in appearance between the two sexes; males are heavier and larger than its female counterpart.

Generally, cats have a heat or estrous cycle, just like any other female creatures and humans. Females are known to be the queen especially when they have their sexual maturity or first heat, which could happen as early as their third or fourth month. Other than that, females have two to three heat cycles during its breeding season, which happens during February to October. However, female cats do not ovulate unless they are bred with males, which mean they are induced ovulators. This scenario increases the chance of conception when breeding.

Chapter Eight: Reproduction in Cats

Signs of Copulation in Cats

There are tell-tale signs that your female cat is in her heat cycle. If these signs are already present, it means that your Tonkinese cat is ready to be mated, and is actively looking for a partner. Male cats know when the females are ready to mate. Here are the signs you need to look out for:

- Rolling, which is a clear sign of flirting
- Rubbing against objects
- Kneading of her back feet
- She will spread her smell or scent, so that the males can smell it
- Makes a long, repeated sound to attract the tom cat.

This behaviour can show for more than 10 days, but still can repeat for more than three months if your cat has not been bread. However, if she has been bred, the cycle will end and her body will prepare for the pregnancy.

If you have bred your female Tonk to a male cat (either they are the same breed or different), you need to expect that the mating process will last for more than ten minutes.

If your queen has already shrieked or screamed loudly, it means that the mating process is done. But you can still mate your cat if she is ready as long as she is still in her

Chapter Eight: Reproduction in Cats

heat cycle. However, if your cat is not ready, she will not pay attention or entertain your male cat, especially if her heat cycle is already done.

The female cat will keep licking herself if she wants to prepare herself for the next mating session. You could mate her again after a few minutes or a few hours. However, it does not really mean that your female cat will mate again with the same male cat; this means that the female cat could produce kittens from different fathers.

If you are not planning to produce kittens, you should keep the male cats from the female one, until the heat cycle is up or until she gives birth. Great indicators of your female cat getting pregnant are her increase in appetite, swollen mammary glands, and large development of her abdomen.

Tips in Handling the Birth Process

When your cat has reached its last two weeks of pregnancy, you need to make sure that you and your family are calm and quiet around your cat. Remind them, especially your children, to handle the car with care.

- o Make your cat inactive and calm during this process, you can buy her a maternity bed for her to lie in or you can offer her a soft bed near a quiet place. Make

Chapter Eight: Reproduction in Cats

sure that your cat has a choice where to give birth and do not move her from her 'spot'

- o Your cat could deliver her own kittens smoothly, however, you should still help her be calm and when she runs into any complications. You can also ask your vet for tips prior to giving birth, the delivering process, and the aftercare that you need to do. If it is possible, also get the number of your vet for assistance. If you ever run into complications, make sure you have a vehicle ready for easy transport to the vet clinic.

- o If you think your cat is already in labor, you need to proper things in advance. These things are clean cloths and towels, clean bowl of warm water, disposal gloves and dental floss, and cat carrier for emergencies. These things are very necessary, so you need to get them immediately!

- o Your cat's labor can be very tricky to know. During the first stages, the female cat will be very restless, pacing around the house as if she is checking or finding something, and sometimes become very noisy.

Chapter Eight: Reproduction in Cats

- o You may call up your vet if you are unsure of the things happening to your cat. You still need to look after your cat if she is nearing her final weeks and days of labour. You need to make sure that you have an estimate when and where she will give birth. Cats love to deliver their babies in private, you only need to observe while she is giving birth and only give a helping hand if there is a problem, or if she is a first time mom.

Stages of Labour and Delivery

Cat labours contain three stages, if you think your cat is already in labour, you need to keep a close eye over the cat. A cat delivery is usually smooth, but you may need to oversee the whole labour process against complications. Again, you do not need to interfere with the process unless really needed, because your cat might be upset or it might slow down the labour. Other than that, limit the people watching the labour process, this too might upset the mother.

Chapter Eight: Reproduction in Cats

Stage 1

- ✓ There is little sign for the first stage, the uterus and cervix are just preparing for delivery.
- ✓ There will be small contractions, but will not be very visible to the naked eye.
- ✓ Restlessness will occur to your cat
- ✓ Your cat will pace around and will become very noisy
- ✓ Your cat will make unproductive trips to her litter box, but will soon settle in her maternity bed.
- ✓ She may choose another spot if she likes to. She might not like to settle in her maternity bed or other spot you have provided her.
- ✓ There will also be vaginal discharge in this stage

Stage 2

- ✓ This stage could last from 2 hours up to 24 hours.
- ✓ Make sure you have everything you needed on hand..
- ✓ Kittens may be born head first or feet first, do not worry because these scenarios are perfectly normal.

Chapter Eight: Reproduction in Cats

- ✓ Some cats will come out every 30 to 45 minutes, but some may come an hour apart.

- ✓ Watch from afar and only intervene if necessary. Some scenarios will include straining but not producing kitten, bloody discharge, passage of kitten very quickly without the mother cleaning the amniotic sacs.

Stage 3

- ✓ The cat placenta will go out after each kitten arrives.

- ✓ You need to carefully count the placenta after each kitten arrives, there should be one placenta per kitten.

- ✓ If there are missing placentas, the mother could have eaten it, or there could be twins. However, you still need to check up with your vet to help you investigate if there are retained placentas inside the body.

- ✓ Cats, sometimes eat some of the placenta, do not worry and be disturbed. You should keep an eye during the birthing process.

Chapter Eight: Reproduction in Cats

Rearing Kittens

Once the kitten has safely arrived, the mother should break the amniotic sac, the thin membrane that embraces the kitten, and clean them thoroughly. It is best that you do not intervene with this process. However, there are instances that the mom may need your help.

You get to help the kittens if the mom does not open the sac, does not do this fully, or does not clean the kitten. Open the sacs carefully using a towel (not a sharp object!), so your kittens can breathe. Next, clean the nose and mouth then dry the kitten with a small clean towel or cloth. You need to rub the kitten firmly using a warm cloth to stimulate the first big breathe. You might need to help the mother bite off or remove the umbilical cord if she is unable to. Using your clean hands or wearing the disposal gloves, tie a dental floss around the cord about two inches from the cat's body, and another away from the body, and cut the umbilical cord between the ties.

Remember, you should not cut the cord too close to the kitten as this will pose great danger to them. However, long ends can be chewed or swallowed by the mom - so make sure you remove them completely! Stop the mom if you see that the mom is chewing the cord too closely to the

Chapter Eight: Reproduction in Cats

kitten. You can still consult your vet in advance if you are worried about cutting the umbilical cord of your cat.

Helping your cat give birth could be quite a breeze, but the delivery will take around two to five hours. Some might even go as long as 24 hours. If you see that the mom is having difficulty in giving birth, you need to contact your vet immediately.

Typically, litters are four to six kittens, some might be lower or higher, but that is not too unusual. If she has already delivered the babies safely, let your cat clean and feed her kittens. Remember, do not intervene with anything, but do not be afraid to handle them and socialize them with you, this is to help you and your cat.

You may need your kitten to your mom's teats if s/he has not suckled from her for more than an hour after being born. You may need to guide the kittens and swap them between teats until they know how to share. You need to consult your vet if the mum is not looking after the kittens, or cleaning, or even feeding them.

These are just some of the essential steps that you need to do if you want to breed your Tonk. It might be an exhausting process, but you can gain a lot of knowledge and money from this one. Make sure you have someone with you to help you in this process.

Chapter Nine: Common Illnesses of Tonkinese Cats

You, now, have a clear idea where to buy your Tonk, how to take care of your Tonk, and how to breed them. It is now time for you to know the common health problem that will affect your Tonk. You need to be aware of the common health problems that may potentially affect your cat, because we all know, prevention is always better than cure. Knowing these things will always be lifesaving to your pet. You need to know how to strengthen your cat's resistance against common illnesses, diseases, and disorders that may affect your cat. Other than this, make sure you have regular check up with the vet to make sure that your cat is always healthy. Remember, your cat will have a happy life if it is healthy!

Chapter Nine: Common Illnesses of Tonkinese Cats

Common Health Problems

In this portion, we will discuss all the diseases that might affect and threaten the health of your Tonkinese cat. Knowing these diseases is vital to you and your cat's overall health. You might even know how to prevent these things if you know them.

Vomiting

- Very common problem not just with cats, but with any other pets.
- There are many causes of vomiting for cats.
- Your cat might have eaten something inedible or poisonous, due to an infection, disease, diabetes or even hair balls.
- This could lead your cat to dehydration, if your cat continues to vomit, call your vet immediately.
- You may need to collect a sample of the vomit for further tests.

Symptoms:

✓ Drooling

✓ Abdominal heaving

Chapter Nine: Common Illnesses of Tonkinese Cats
Feline Lower Urinary Tract Diseases (FLUTD)

- As high as 3% of cats have this disease
- Both female and male cats can get FLUTD
- This disease occurs to the cats that are unfit, overweight, or eat too much dry food
- You can raise your cat's risk of FLUTD due to stress, sudden changes, and multi-cat household.
- Treatment depends on the case or the scenario of the cat.
- You should contact your vet immediately if your cat has problem in urinating.

Symptoms:

- ✓ Straining to urinate
- ✓ Bloody urine
- ✓ Licking around the urinary area (often because of pain)
- ✓ Depression
- ✓ Dehydration
- ✓ Crying when urinating
- ✓ Lack of appetite
- ✓ Vomiting
- ✓ Urinating in unusual places

Chapter Nine: Common Illnesses of Tonkinese Cats

Fleas

- Common external feline problem
- It is very easy to treat
- Your cat could have anemia if the fleas live for more than a year on your cat.
- Make sure you have completely eradicated your cat's fleas
- Ask your vet for the correct treatment for your cat. Some treatment includes: powder, foams, topical, and oral medication.

Signs that your cat has fleas:

✓ Red or irritated skin

✓ Hair loss

✓ Constant scratching

✓ Frequent licking

✓ Skin infections or hot spots

✓ Flea dirt on its skin (they look like tiny black dots)

Chapter Nine: Common Illnesses of Tonkinese Cats

Tapeworms

- Another common feline health problem
- Tapeworms live inside your kitten's small intestine and could grow as large as two feet.
- These tapeworms are segmented but break apart when expelled.
- Look at your cat's feces and anus to see if your cat has tapeworms.
- Tapeworms come out of the cat's anus when sleeping or relax.
- Your cat could have tapeworms due to fleas, so make sure you eradicate the flea problem.

Symptoms:

- ✓ Vomiting
- ✓ Weight loss

Quick Treatment:

- ✓ Topical medication
- ✓ Oral medication
- ✓ Injection

Chapter Nine: Common Illnesses of Tonkinese Cats

Diarrhea

- There are many things that cause diarrhea, such as intestinal parasite, allergies, liver disease, spoiled food, infection, and etc.
- Offer fresh, clean water to prevent dehydration if your cat has diarrhea.
- Remove the food immediately after s/he has eaten it.
- Take your cat immediately to the vet if you notice vomiting, bloody, or dark stools, with fever, lethargy, loss of appetite and difficulty in pooping.

Symptom includes:

✓ Loose watery stool that could last for a day, week, or even months.

Eye Problems

- Some causes of eye problems are cataracts, trauma, inflammation, conjunctivitis, glaucoma, and retinal disease.
- Call your vet immediately if you saw these symptoms because these problems are very difficult to treat.

Chapter Nine: Common Illnesses of Tonkinese Cats

Symptoms include:

- ✓ Watery eyes
- ✓ Cloudiness in vision
- ✓ Read or white eyelid lining
- ✓ Gunk in corners of the eye
- ✓ Tear-stained fur
- ✓ Squinting
- ✓ Pawing
- ✓ Visible third eyelid.

Chapter Nine: Common Illnesses of Tonkinese Cats

Quick Summary and Care Sheet

You now possess the needed knowledge for owning your first Tonkinese cat. Why not practice your knowledge and put it to the test? There are still a lot of things you need to know about our furry companion, you can still search it online for more information about the breed. There are still great ways to make them happy and healthy in the comfort of your own home. Aside from this, we hope that you will become a reputable breeder soon enough.

In this last chapter, we will give you a quick guide in taking care of your own Tonkinese cat. Think of it as your own, "cheat sheet". This will enable you to find the information you need if you are in a hurry.

Biological and Historical Data

Origin: United States of America, Canada, Thailand

Pedigree: crossbreed of Siamese and Burmese

Breed Size: medium – size breed

Body Type and Appearance: Has a firm

Group: Cat Fanciers' Association (CFA), Fédération Internationale Féline (FIFe), The International Cat Association (TICA), Australian Cat Federation (ACF), Canadian Cat Association (CCA – AFC).

Height: 8 to 10 inches

Weight: average of 6 – 12 pounds

Coat Length: short ticked coat

Coat Texture: fine, silky, smooth, and soft

Color: brown, blue, platinum and, champagne (a paler shade of buff-beige). While European standards accept fawn, tortoiseshell, cinnamon, red, caramel, cream, and apricot.

Temperament: friendly, active, loving, demands attention, affectionate, involved in all activities, and likes to meet people

Strangers: friendly around strangers

Other Cats: if properly trained, introduced and socialized, they are generally good

Other Pets: friendly with other pets

Training: very trainable, clever, and responsive

Exercise Needs: does not need any special exercise, likes to play with toys and games

Health Conditions: generally healthy but could contract gingivitis, feline inflammatory bowel disease, excessive protein in body organs, upper respiratory infection, and etc.

Lifespan: average 10 to 16 years

Keeping Tonkinese Cats

United States: There is no strict federal requirement in licensing cats or dogs. Some may be regulated at state level.

United Kingdom: You need to get a special permit if you want to ravel with your cat in and outside of the country. However, pets are still subject to quarantine.

Other countries: Bring the necessary documents for your cat. These documents are the vaccinations, rabies certificate to show health condition. However, there are still requirements per country.

Selecting the Right Tonkinese Cat

Where to Purchase: Online Stores, Backyard/Private Breeders, Cat Conventions or Pet Conferences

Characteristics of a Reputable Breeder: A reputable breeder will ask you questions about yourself. Aside from this, you can ask a lot of things from the breeder and you can expect that she or he knows the answer.

Characteristics of a Healthy Breed: Examine your pet's body thoroughly. You may want to start from the eyes up to tail. Aside from the physical characteristics, your cat should be playful and active, especially with the other members of the litter. Any sign of lethargy is a big no-no!

Habitat Requirements for Tonkinese Cats: You may need to provide a big bed for your pet, because your cat may grow bigger overtime. Other than that, you may need to provide toys, perches, play pen, treats, and other accessories.

Housing Temperature: your house should be at normal temperature, not too hot or too cold.

Essential Nutrients for Tonkinese Cat

- Tonks are naturally carnivorous animals. Make sure you give them more protein and meat that the veggies that you usually give your dog.

How to Feed Your Cat: You may want to consult your vet on how to properly feed your cat. However, you can do the trial and error method and test what kind of feeding measurement your Tonk would want.

Feeding Amount/Frequency: There are a lot of factors affecting the feeding amount and frequency, these are age, energy levels, previous conditions, size, weight etc. You may want to consult your vet to make sure that your cat will get the best food possible.

Grooming Tips

How to Brush Your Cat's Teeth: Brush your cat's teeth daily, if it cannot, you can do it twice a week first.

How to Trim Your Cat's Nails: Trim your cat's nail once a week or twice a month. You may need to practice this habit first, though.

Cleaning Your Cat's Ears: Remove the normal wax build-up using a cat ear cleaning solution and squeeze a few drops in the ear canal. However, you just do this occasionally.

It is still ideal to clean your cat's ears occasionally just to

Showing Tips for Your Tonkinese Cats

- Must appear enthusiastic, lively and active
- Must be a colorful cat with a ticked coat
- Must be medium – size should show a hard and muscular body structure
- Should be physically, and temperamentally well – balanced
- Must have pass the specific requirements of the breed standard.

(Look up Breed Standard in Chapter 7 for complete list)

Glossary of Cat Terms

Abundism – Referring to a cat that has markings more prolific than is normal.

Acariasis – A type of mite infection.

ACF – Australian Cat Federation

Affix – A cattery name that follows the cat's registered name; cattery owner, not the breeder of the cat.

Agouti – A type of natural coloring pattern in which individual hairs have bands of light and dark coloring.

Ailurophile – A person who loves cats.

Albino – A type of genetic mutation which results in little to no pigmentation, in the eyes, skin, and coat.

Allbreed – Referring to a show that accepts all breeds or a judge who is qualified to judge all breeds.

Alley Cat – A non-pedigreed cat.

Alter – A desexed cat; a male cat that has been neutered or a female that has been spayed.

Amino Acid – The building blocks of protein; there are 22 types for cats, 11 of which can be synthesized and 11 which must come from the diet (see essential amino acid).

Anestrus – The period between estrus cycles in a female cat.

Any Other Variety (AOV) – A registered cat that doesn't conform to the breed standard.

ASH – American Shorthair, a breed of cat.

Back Cross – A type of breeding in which the offspring is mated back to the parent.

Balance – Referring to the cat's structure; proportional in accordance with the breed standard.

Barring – Describing the tabby's striped markings.

Base Color – The color of the coat.

Bicolor – A cat with patched color and white.

Blaze – A white coloring on the face, usually in the shape of an inverted V.

Bloodline – The pedigree of the cat.

Brindle – A type of coloring, a brownish or tawny coat with streaks of another color.

Castration – The surgical removal of a male cat's testicles.

Cat Show – An event where cats are shown and judged.

Cattery – A registered cat breeder; also, a place where cats may be boarded.

CFA – The Cat Fanciers Association.

Cobby – A compact body type.

Colony – A group of cats living wild outside.

Color Point – A type of coat pattern that is controlled by color point alleles; pigmentation on the tail, legs, face, and ears with an ivory or white coat.

Colostrum – The first milk produced by a lactating female; contains vital nutrients and antibodies.

Conformation – The degree to which a pedigreed cat adheres to the breed standard.

Cross Breed – The offspring produced by mating two distinct breeds.

Dam – The female parent.

Declawing – The surgical removal of the cat's claw and first toe joint.

Developed Breed – A breed that was developed through selective breeding and crossing with established breeds.

Down Hairs – The short, fine hairs closest to the body which keep the cat warm.

DSH – Domestic Shorthair.

Estrus – The reproductive cycle in female cats during which she becomes fertile and receptive to mating.

Fading Kitten Syndrome – Kittens that die within the first two weeks after birth; the cause is generally unknown.

Feral – A wild, untamed cat of domestic descent.

Gestation – Pregnancy; the period during which the fetuses develop in the female's uterus.

Guard Hairs – Coarse, outer hairs on the coat.

Harlequin – A type of coloring in which there are van markings of any color with the addition of small patches of the same color on the legs and body.

Inbreeding – The breeding of related cats within a closed group or breed.

Kibble – Another name for dry cat food.

Lilac – A type of coat color that is pale pinkish-gray.

Line – The pedigree of ancestors; family tree.

Litter – The name given to a group of kittens born at the same time from a single female.

Mask – A type of coloring seen on the face in some breeds.

Matts – Knots or tangles in the cat's fur.

Mittens – White markings on the feet of a cat.

Moggie – Another name for a mixed breed cat.

Mutation – A change in the DNA of a cell.

Muzzle – The nose and jaws of an animal.

Natural Breed – A breed that developed without selective breeding or the assistance of humans.

Neutering – Desexing a male cat.

Open Show – A show in which spectators are allowed to view the judging.

Pads – The thick skin on the bottom of the feet.

Particolor – A type of coloration in which there are markings of two or more distinct colors.

Patched – A type of coloration in which there is any solid color, tabby, or tortoiseshell color plus white.

Pedigree – A purebred cat; the cat's papers showing its family history.

Pet Quality – A cat that is not deemed of high enough standard to be shown or bred.

Piebald – A cat with white patches of fur.

Points – Also color points; markings of contrasting color on the face, ears, legs, and tail.

Pricked – Referring to ears that sit upright.

Purebred – A pedigreed cat.

Queen – An intact female cat.

Roman Nose – A type of nose shape with a bump or arch.

Scruff – The loose skin on the back of a cat's neck.

Selective Breeding – A method of modifying or improving a breed by choosing cats with desirable traits.

Senior – A cat that is more than 5 but less than 7 years old.

Sire – The male parent of a cat.

Solid – Also self; a cat with a single coat color.

Spay – Desexing a female cat.

Stud – An intact male cat.

Tabby – A type of coat pattern consisting of a contrasting color over a ground color.

Tom Cat – An intact male cat.

Tortoiseshell – A type of coat pattern consisting of a mosaic of red or cream and another base color.

Tri-Color – A type of coat pattern consisting of three distinct colors in the coat.

Tuxedo – A black and white cat.

Unaltered – A cat that has not been desexed.

Index

A

amino acid 109
antibodies 111

B

bed 77
body 111, 112
breed 110, 111, 112, 113, 114
breeder 109, 110
breeding 110, 111, 112, 113

C

Cat Fanciers Association 111
cattery 109
CFA 111
claw 111
coat 7, 102, 109, 110, 111, 112, 114
color 110, 111, 112, 113, 114
cycle 112

D

desexed 109, 114
diet 109
DNA 113
domestic 112

E

ears	111, 113
essential	109
estrus	110

F

face	110, 111, 112, 113
family	112, 113
feet	112, 113
female	109, 110, 111, 112, 114
fertile	112
food	77, 112
fur	112, 113

G

genetic	109

I

infection	109
intact	114

J

judge	109

K

kittens	112

L

lactating 111

M

male 109, 110, 113, 114
markings 109, 110, 112, 113
milk 111
mite 109
mutation 109

N

neutered 109
nose 113, 114
nutrients 111

O

offspring 110, 111

P

pattern 109, 111, 114
pedigree 110, 112
pets 8, 103
pigmentation 109, 111
protein 109
purebred 113

S

show 109, 113
skin 109, 113, 114
standard 110, 111, 113

T

tail 111, 113
traits 114

Photo Credits

Page 1 Photo by user Stephen Lloyd-Smart via Flickr.com, https://www.flickr.com/photos/thenaturephotographer/40403983331/

Page 4 Photo by user Julicath/Cath via Flickr.com, https://www.flickr.com/photos/9221141@N02/2295247019/

Page 11 Photo by user Barb Henry via Flickr.com, https://www.flickr.com/photos/bhenry/40342954/

Page 27 Photo by user Frank Roche via Flickr.com, https://www.flickr.com/photos/orchidthief/50469621/

Page 43 Photo by user Julicath/Cath via Flickr.com, https://www.flickr.com/photos/9221141@N02/3207099244/

Page 52 Photo by user Julicath/Cath via Flickr.com, https://www.flickr.com/photos/9221141@N02/3406881038/

Page 61 Photo by user iampeas via Flickr.com, https://www.flickr.com/photos/iampeas/4367133994/

Page 70 Photo by user Evan Balbier via Flickr.com, https://www.flickr.com/photos/evnhunter/4301992633/

Page 80 Photo by user Angela Thomas via Flickr.com, https://www.flickr.com/photos/anyaka/753701485/

Page 91 Photo by Francis Mariani user via Flickr.com, https://www.flickr.com/photos/designwallah/4513020178/

Page 99 Photo by user Tomcio77 via Flickr.com, https://www.flickr.com/photos/tomcio77/4577058802/

References

"About the Tonkinese" – Cat Fancier's Organization

http://cfa.org/Breeds/BreedsSthruT/Tonkinese.aspx

"Tonkinese Origins & A Brief History"- Tonkinese.me

http://www.tonkinese.me/tonkinese-history.html

"Tonkinese" - VetStreet.com

http://www.vetstreet.com/cats/tonkinese#1_60cabv22

"Tonkinese Cat Problems" – Written by Amy Armstrong via TheNest.com

https://pets.thenest.com/tonkinese-cat-problems-4692.html

"Tonkinese" - PetMD.com

https://www.petmd.com/cat/breeds/c_ct_tonkinese#

"Pro's & Cons of the Tonkienese Catdog" – Wixsite.com

http://tonkinese.wixsite.com/tonkanees/single-post/2014/03/23/Pros-Cons-of-the-Tonkinese-Catdog

"Tonkinese Cat Profile – History, Appearance & Temperament"- Cat – World.com

https://www.cat-world.com.au/tonkinese-breed-profile.html#History:

"Tonkinese" – CatTime.com

http://cattime.com/cat-breeds/tonkinese-cats#/slide/1

"Cat-Proof Your Home with 12 Easy Tips" - HumaneSociety.org

http://www.humanesociety.org/animals/cats/tips/cat_proofing_your_house.html

"What Foods to Feed Your New Tonkinese" – AnimalCareTip.com

http://animalcaretip.com/what-foods-to-feed-your-new-tonkinese/

"A Simple Guide to Feeding Your Cat" – CatDoctors.info

http://catdoctors.info/simple-guide-feeding-cat/

"6 Most Common Cat Health Problems" – WebMD.com

https://pets.webmd.com/cats/6-most-common-cat-health-problems

"Common Cat Diseases" – ASPCA.org

https://www.aspca.org/pet-care/cat-care/common-cat-diseases

"Labour and Giving Birth" – Purina.co.uk

https://www.purina.co.uk/cats/key-life-stages/pregnancy/cat-labour-and-giving-birth

"Nutrition - Feeding Guidelines for Cats" – Written by Ernest Ward, DVM via VCAHospitals.com

https://vcahospitals.com/know-your-pet/nutrition-feeding-guidelines-for-cats